I0414704

YOUNG MAN VIEW
ON THE WORLD

MAA ZHI HONG

FIRST EDITION

FOREWORD FROM THE AUTHOR

If you are reading this book right now, I would like to express a big thank you to you! Thank you for taking your precious time to read this book as it meant a great deal to me. Writing current affairs commentaries for the newspaper is something which I didn't expect and it is so surreal till today. It has been one heck of a ride and I look forward to producing more articles and books to benefit the world in the future.

Publishing all these articles into a book format is also another dream realized for me.

All the articles which you are about to read had not been easy to write. I poured my heart and soul into each article to provide the best coherent analysis I can give for the situation described in the article. Granted, you may disagree with the analysis and it is normal. After all, it is opinion-based and everyone has the right to have their own opinions.

I know I have more room for improvement and I will continue to work hard to improve myself. This is just the beginning of my long writing career and I look forward to learning from renowned experts around the

MAA ZHI HONG

world.

SPECIAL THANKS TO THOSE WHO MATTERS

Special thanks to my parents and sister for their support and love in all these years. Without them, I would not be the person I am today.

To my mentors Eddy and Steven, thank you for your guidance and advice given to me in the past few years.

I would also like to thank Jason Tan, Associate Editor of TODAY Singapore for giving me a chance to contribute articles to TODAY Singapore. Without my early foundation with TODAY, it would be impossible for me to be in the present position I am in.

I would like to give my heartfelt thanks to editor of Asia Times, David Simmons, for granting me the permission to republish my Asia Times articles. Without his consent, this book would not have existed.

A big thanks to Amos and Jerald for your brotherhood and friendship.

There are just simply too many people to thank and I expressed my apologies to those who are not explicitly acknowledged. I want you to know I am grateful to each and everyone of you.

THIS IS MY FIRST
BOOK AND THERE
WILL BE MANY
MORE NEW BOOKS
IN THE FUTURE!

BIOGRAPHY OF
THE AUTHOR

Hi, I am 22 years old this year and I live in Singapore. Unlike many authors, I don't have a degree from a university and I don't hold big positions in government and business.

The only "degree" I have is determination and I savored online articles on a daily basis.

I have been reading current affairs news since the age of 11 , and while boys at my age were watching cartoons, I was busy reading newspapers.

Those early years of reading form the basis of my perspective of the world which we live in today.

To know more about me, you are welcome to follow me at @maazhihongofficial on Instagram.

PAKATAN HARAPAN MUST NOT REST ON ITS LAURELS

MAY 6, 2019

Pakatan Harapan's Mahathir Mohamad (R) addresses a press conference after the general election, in Petaling Jaya, Malaysia, on May 9, 2018. Photo: Reuters

On the night of May 9, 2018, Malaysians of all political affiliations could not believe their eyes as they processed the election results coming in after polling had ended. After all, Prime Minister Najib Razak had done his best to stack the deck in his favor; he gerrymandered the electoral system to give heavier weight to rural Malaysia, which had backed his coalition in the 2013 general election.

In the end, all of this came to naught.

One by one, many senior Barisan Nasional (BN) ministers lost their seats to the opposition.

One example is the parliamentary seat of Muar in Johor, where BN's deputy minister in the prime minister's department, Razali Ibrahim, lost his seat by a margin of 7,000 votes to Pakatan's Syed Saddiq.

Syed Saddiq later rose to become one of the youngest ministers in Malaysian history, assuming the portfolio of youth and sports.

After it became clear that BN had lost the election, there were fears within the country that then premier Najib Razak might resort to unscrupulous methods to subvert the election results.

It wasn't until Dr Mahathir Mohamad was sworn in as PM at Istana Negara the day after the election that things started to stabilize within the country.

Since Pakatan Harapan took power, it had enjoyed a honeymoon with the Malaysian public, who were largely disgusted by the excesses of the previous government. The new government's initial move to repeal the GST and restart the stalled investigation into the 1MDB scandal helped the new government to entrench its popularity with the public.

Many Malaysians had viewed the 2018 general election as a chance for the country to start anew and move forward to a better future

Many Malaysians had viewed the 2018 general election as a chance for the country to start anew and move forward to a better future. The level of optimism was so high that there was a news report about Malaysians working in neighboring Singapore quitting their jobs to move back to their motherland.

However, as the Pakatan Harapan government nears its one-year anniversary in power, there are clear warning signs that things are not going well.

According to the latest survey done by Merdeka Center, only 39% of voters were satisfied with the government and 46% of voters felt the country was on the wrong path.

The discontent has translated to a string of defeats in the by-election for the PH government, so it should pay heed to the lessons offered by the former Democratic Party of Japan (DPJ) government(2009-2012).

Like the PH in Malaysia, the DPJ defeated the long-ruling Liberal Democratic of Party of Japan (LDP) in a landslide victory in 2009 by promising Japanese voters a series of changes. Unfortunately, the DPJ failed to achieve most of its reform agenda and legislative productivity fell to a historic low level despite its overwhelming majority in the lower house. There was infighting within the DPJ government, which further dented its popularity. In the end, the DPJ was tossed out in the next election and the political change of 2009 is now viewed as party change without policy change.

Similarly, here in Malaysia, the PH government has backpedaled on many of its campaign promises. It bowed to conservative Malay pressures and decided not to sign up to the Elimination of All Forms of Racial Discrimination (ICERD) This has disappointed many Malaysian liberals who had voted for PH.

PH failure to recognize exam certificates from Independent Chinese Schools risks undermining its strong support among the Malaysian Chinese whose defection in 2008 and 2013 led to Barisan Nasional's loss of its crucial two-thirds majority.

And there are also signs that the PH government is not as cohesive as it should be. One notable example is the underlying tension between Economic Minister Azmin Ali and premier-in-waiting Anwar Ibrahim. Acceptance of the former government members into the party of Prime Minister Mahathir Mohamad has not gone down well with the coalition partners in PH.

This has led to Nurul Izzah Anwar quitting her party posts and stating that she has lost faith in the Mahathir government in an interview with The Straits Times. Such infighting reflects badly on the government and risks widening fissures within the coalition.

Lastly, the political instability and external events have led to the weakening of investor confidence in the Malaysian economy, which has dented support for the government. The World Bank projects that the rate of Malaysia's annual GDP growth will drop below what it was in 2015 should current trends continue.

Hence, as PH celebrates its first anniversary, it should not be resting on its laurels. But rather it should take a hard look at itself and contemplate a new direction forward.

The PH government should get its houses in order and focus on fulfilling its promises to the voters instead of bickering among themselves. It should also be prepared to implement unpopular structural reforms to

boost long-term international confidence in the Malaysian economy.
Prime Minister Mahathir should also announce and be committed to a clear public timeline for Anwar Ibrahim to succeed him. This will clear all lingering doubts over the succession plan and avoid giving opportunists a chance to sow discord in the coalition. Malaysia needs certainty from the government and the government must demonstrate that it can provide it.

Only by taking these steps can the PH government address the problem of uncertainty and demonstrate that it is a viable and functioning government that can steer Malaysia in a new direction. Then the PH government can show that it is different from its predecessor. If not, PH risks repeating the mistakes of its DPJ counterpart in Japan in the next election.

TRUMP, CHINA AND THE ART OF NO DEAL

MAY 15, 2019

US President Donald Trump came into office on a campaign promise to correct what he had perceived to be one-sided trade deals. He promised voters on the campaign trail that he would exercise his business acumen to great effect in the White House. Trump repeatedly said he would negotiate great deals that would benefit American workers and companies. He targeted countries like South Korea, Japan and China for running large trade surpluses with the US.

Fortunately, my country, Singapore, ran a large trade deficit with the US. Hence Singapore has been spared Trump's wrath and avoided getting hit with tariffs that would have a devastating impact on the island state.

However, Trump's trade war against China has unnerved global markets and is bound to have untold consequences for the entire world. The global trading system that we know of today was established by the United States after the end of World War II, and Washington has helped to build institutions such as the World Trade Organization (WTO) and the World Bank to foster a rules-based trading system that has benefited the entire world.

Now the global trading system is under unprecedented assault and if this continues it is bound to have grievous global consequences.

Trump recently upped the ante in his trade war with China by escalating tariffs on US$200 billion worth of Chinese goods from 10% to 25%. While many pundits have said Trump is not in a rush to make a deal, the actions he has taken that the opposite is true.

Trump desperately needs a trade deal with China as he gears up for his re-election bid in 2020.

His gambit to conclude a deal with North Korea collapsed in failure in Hanoi in February, and it is a huge blow to his self-styled image of a master dealmaker. Trump also faces a flurry of congressional subpoenas at home from Democrats who now control the House of Representatives. Hence with mounting legal and political troubles, Trump is cornered and desperately needs a conclusion to the prolonged trade war with China, which has net-ted zero benefits for him.

The prospect of a trade deal with China remains as elusive as ever, despite Trump's increased tariffs to pressure China to come to the negotiating table with the list of concession that he wants. It is highly unlikely that China will grant Trump the concessions he wants. China remembers clearly the deal that Tokyo concluded with Washington in the 1990s that caused Japan to slip into economic stagnation for many years. That period has now been dubbed Japan's "lost decade."

China is not dumb and it will not concede to Trump.

Worse still, the move to increase tariffs took place while Chinese Vice-Premier Liu He was in Washington to negotiate with the Trump administration.

It is a blunder by Trump and will be perceived by the Chinese as a cheap shot against President Xi Jinping. The tariffs hike came despite Xi's "beautiful letter" to Trump, and it is a massive loss of face for the Chinese leader to see his group of officials return home from Washington with no deal to conclude the trade war.

Xi could not afford to look weak in front of his people and

he knows that millions of Chinese netizens access information about the outside world by using virtual private networks (VPNs) to circumvent the Great Firewall. Many ordinary Chinese know about the trade war's latest developments and should any deal with Trump infringe on China's core interests, it will be political suicide for Xi.

One of the main reasons the US-China trade talks broke down was that Washington's demands were unpalatable to China. Some of the demands from the US, such as an end to government support for state companies in specific industries and a streamlined approval process for genetically engineered US crops, are a direct challenge to the Communist Party of China's control of the economy.

Since Xi took office, he has extended the party's reach into every corner of Chinese society, and every businessman in China who aspires to reach the top of the hierarchy knows that they must receive the blessing of the party. It is not surprising that even Jack Ma, who is one of China's most internationally recognizable figures, has been revealed to be a member of the CPC after years of denial.

Hence in the face of renewed pressure from Trump, Xi and the Chinese government have reached the conclusion that it is better to bear the consequences of increased tariffs than to concede to US demands.

Xi is in for the long haul and can well afford to ride out the storm. And based on Trump's past negotiations such as his failed bid to pressure House Democrats to fund his wall on the Mexican border, which led to the longest government shutdown in US history, Xi knows that the chances are good that Trump will blink first.

As for Trump, the protracted trade war has hurt his base in the swing states that voted for him in 2016 over Hillary Clinton. There will be a point where the costs to American voters will be so great that the US political establishment will pressure Trump to change his approach on China.

Xi only has to harden his stance and not concede. Sooner or later, Trump will come back to the table and relax his demands.

It is only a matter of time before Trump will once again expose himself as a man of the art of no deal.

HOW XI AND ABE CAN BRIDGE CHINA-JAPAN DIVIDE

MAY 16, 2019

Japan's Prime Minister Shinzo Abe, left, shakes hands with China's President Xi Jinping in Beijing on October 26, 2018. Photo: AFP

Chinese President Xi Jinping and Japanese Prime Minister Shinzo Abe have much more in common than they may realize. Both come from elite political families with great influence within their respective countries.

Xi is considered a princeling within China because he is the son of Xi Zhongxun, who was one of the founding fathers of the People's Republic of China. Abe is a third-generation politician, following in the footsteps of both his grandfather and his father.

Both men took over the top political job in their countries in late 2012. Xi succeeded Hu Jintao to be the general secretary of the Communist Party of China and Abe, who had served as prime minister from 2006-07, stormed back to the premiership in a landslide election victory.

Both have presided over assertive foreign policies since assuming office. Xi spoke about a rejuvenated China and vowed to protect its core interests when necessary, and in 2013 he even declared an Air Defense Identification Zone in the East China Sea. Abe, for his part, vowed to amend the country's pacifist constitution by 2020 and successfully pushed through a reinterpretation of the constitution's Article 9 to give the Japanese Self-Defense Forces more leeway during combat.

With all that said, why have Japan and China, led by men who are quite similar, failed to develop a smooth relationship? The two countries' relations have yet to be fully restored to what they were before the dispute over the Senkaku/Diaoyu Islands deepened. The recent rapprochement between Xi and Abe is more of a pragmatic move as both squared off with US President Donald Trump over trade policy.

Historically, the relationship between the two Asian neighbors has been colored by China's bitter memories of Japanese occupation during World War II. However, they have since strived to keep the relationship on an even keel for the greater good.

But the nature of the relationship has changed since 2012, when the Japanese government moved to nationalize the Senkakus, which the Chinese call the Diaoyus, reawakening a dispute that had rumbled on relatively quietly for decades. The nationalization move serves to escalate the dispute significantly and laid the groundwork for today's rocky relationship.

The governor of Tokyo at that time, Shintaro Ishihara, had announced plans to purchase the islands from their private owners and assert Japanese sovereignty over them. The central government was worried that he would incite a conflict with China and decided to pre-empt him by getting its own hands on the islands first.

What the government probably didn't expect was the ferocity of the reaction from Beijing. China has claimed the islands as its own and named them Diaoyu Dao.

The nationalization move was widely seen in China as an insult, and no Chinese leader could afford to look weak in front of their domestic audience. A hardline stance toward Japan was the only plausible choice. And the nationalization of the islands came just before Xi's ascension to power, and he could not afford to play nice.

In Japan, the aversion to China resulting from its growing economic and military might has grown dramatically over the years, which provides fertile ground for right-wing leaders like Abe to thrive

. He was left to deal with the Senkakus mess left by the previous Democratic Party of Japan government and he could not afford to back down in light of repeated Chinese incursions around the islands.

The Sino-Japanese relationship remained in a subdued state for years.

So how can Japan and China get out of this mess? First, there are encouraging signs of a thaw in the relationship.

On April 24 in Beijing, Liberal Democratic Party (LDP) Secretary-

General Toshihiro Nikai was warmly received by Xi. Nikai passed a letter from Abe to Xi that called for a fresh era in the Sino-Japanese relationship. The letter came against the backdrop of Abe's own visit to China in October 2018, the first by a Japanese prime minister in six years. Xi also agreed to travel to Japan in June for the G20 summit.

While it is encouraging that the relationship has been warming again, this has happened in the past, but then the relationship went off track again. There is a need to ensure the relationship is put on the right track for the long term.

For the sake of the future of their countries and the region, Xi and Abe should muster the courage to build more goodwill between their countries and ensure the thaw in their relationship lasts.

Xi and Abe are both strongmen in their respective countries and only they have the political strength to take steps to restore the bilateral relationship.

China and Japan should continue to deepen economic interlinks with each other and cultural exchanges between their people to deepen people-to-people ties to promote mutual understanding.

Abe should emulate the example set by Emperor Emeritus Akihito in acknowledging the damage done by Japan during World War II.

Most Japanese don't subscribe to the right-wing beliefs held by Abe's conservative base. Abe can still respect the war dead in Japan without being associated with the Yasukuni Shrine. By doing so, he will give leaders in China and South Korea space to tone down their hardline stance toward Japan and set a new era of cooperation.

Abe should widen his political appeal to the center of Japanese politics, and by doing so, he will build an alternative source of power to leverage on and enable him to sustain this new approach should he opt for it without being held hostage to the right-wing base. Abe can secure a new legacy in Japan as the leader who has finally made peace with China. He wants to restore Japan to being a "normal" country and wants to enhance Japan's security. But his move is fiercely opposed by neighboring countries.

The only reason China fiercely opposed Japan's attempt to amend its pacifist constitution was that it still perceived Japan to be insufficiently apologetic for its crimes during World War II.

Unlike Japan, Germany came to terms with its World War II past and now has been accepted by its European neighbors. Germany is able to maintain a normal army and be accepted on the continent as a peer.

Improving the relationship with China is one indispensable component should Abe and his faction want to succeed in amending the Japanese constitution.

Xi, on the other hand, should do more to reassure Japan about its concerns over national security. Xi must be more mindful of how he has been exercising China power and how it has been perceived by neighboring countries. Building a moderate image in Japan will not give oxygen to the right-wingers to sustain their power in Japan. This will pave the way for moderate centrist leaders to assume prominence in Japanese politics.

Slowly but steadily, the relationship between the two countries can be restored one day. The future of the Sino-Japanese relationship depends on the countries' leaders.

INDONESIA MUST ADDRESS CREEPING ISLAMIZATION

MAY 17, 2019

Indonesian President Joko Widodo. Photo: AFP/Donal Husni/Nur Photo

This month marks the 21st anniversary of the infamous anti-Chinese riots in Indonesia that killed thousands and caused many Chinese to flee abroad to places like Taiwan, China, Singapore and Australia.

The fact that the anniversary of this infamous incident was marked peacefully is a key indicator of the extraordinary progress made by Indonesia since the fall of President Suharto in 1998.

When Suharto fell from power shortly after the deadly anti-Chinese riots, the world was anxious about Indonesia. Many feared that the country, which is one of the most culturally and ethnically diverse nations in the world, would be torn apart, leading to chaos. Many wondered how a country that had been held together by brute force could remain intact under a democratic system.

Fortunately for Indonesia, it has proved the cynical pundits wrong.

Post-Suharto Indonesia succeeded in remaining united as one nation because of Jakarta's wise decision to devolve power to the regions. This enabled each region within the country to exercise the power to decide how to deal with their local issues while leaving national issues to the central government in Jakarta. This helped to calm tensions between the regions and the central government that had been rising since Suharto came to power.

Had Jakarta insisted on continuing with the Suharto-era model of centralized governance, there is a chance the country would indeed have balkanized. Regional autonomy saved Indonesia.

Another factor behind Indonesia's tremendous progress is the Pancasila ideology, which stipulates that there is no state religion. All citizens are allowed to practice their own religion and all religions are respected by the state. This helped to keep the Muslim-majority but religiously diverse country stay together.

However, in spite of all this, there are clear warning signs for Indonesia moving forward. And if they are not addressed, Indonesia risks going down the path of Turkey.

It has been clear to the outside world for some time that there has been an alarming rise in the politicization of Islam by many politicians in Indonesia. One of the best examples is the downfall of former Jakarta governor Ahok after a doctored video circulated online of him remarking on a verse in the Koran. It led to a public outcry despite there being proof that the video was faked. Ahok's opponents launched a campaign to tell voters that Ahok disrespected Islam. In the end, Ahok was defeated and the Indonesian court jailed the ex-governor on charges of blasphemy in May 2017. It was a verdict that was harsher than what prosecutors had requested – a suspended jail sentence on account of Ahok's "huge contribution" to the capital city.

The person who doctored the video was jailed for six months and later for 18 months. This proved that Ahok's conviction was unjust, but the Indonesian judicial system did not overturn his verdict. This illustrates the tremendous pressure being exerted by the Islamist groups that have emerged since 1998.

President Jokowi's choice of Ma'ruf Amin as his running mate is another sign that political Islam is on the rise.

Ma'ruf Amin is the spiritual leader of Nahdlatul Ulama (NU), which is the largest Muslim organization both in Indonesia and the world. He is one of the key figures behind Ahok's downfall in 2017 and wields great influence over many devout Muslim voters.

President Joko Widodo, widely known as Jokowi, was shaken by the downfall of Ahok in 2017 and quickly moved to build closer ties with figures like Ma'ruf Amin to secure conservative votes.

The president made a strategic move to select Ma'ruf Amin to blunt the accusation that he has been anti-Islam, and he even flew to Mecca days before the vote to show Indonesian voters that he is a devout Muslim. This was necessary in the face of fierce campaigning by his opponent, former general Prabowo, who had played up his Islamic credentials.

In the end, Jokowi prevailed but at a great cost. He abandoned his previous moderate position, disappointing many of his liberal supporters. Minorities in Indonesia are uncertain about their future but decided to stick to Jokowi as the alternative is unacceptable to many of them. Many still remember the role played by Prabowo in the 1998 crisis, though he has denied any role in it. This came against the backdrop of decades of mainstream religious exclusivism in Indonesian politics. President Jokowi's re-election is more of a respite than a triumphant scenario for Indonesia

Now moving forward, it is the norm for candidates to prove how "Islamic" they are to voters, as it is the basis for determining their suitability for high office. It is difficult for moderate Muslim candidates to win if they do not play the religiosity game.

Indonesia should consider Turkey, which used to be a secular nation but is currently under the rule of an Islamist, Recep Tayyip Erdogan, who was jailed by the previous government before he came to power in 2004. Since Erdogan came to power, he has steadily reversed the secular position of the state and repealed policies such as a ban on wearing headscarves in public universities. The founder of modern Turkey, Mustafa Kemal Atatürk, believed very strongly in the separation of state and religion, which he enshrined in Turkey's governing ideology – Kemalism.

Today in Erdogan's Turkey, Kemalism exists only in name. It has lost potency as Islamization has taken root. This has led to a bitter divide between those who believe in Kemalism and those who want Turkey to embrace Islam, who make up the bulk of Erdogan's support base.

But Turkey still stays together as one nation because the people share a common identity – their nation-state is the successor to the Ottoman empire. Indonesia, on the other hand, is ethnically and religiously diverse, so there is a risk of balkanization.

It is high time for Indonesia's leaders to take a stand and address creeping Islamization before it is too late.

HUAWEI SAGA IS PRELUDE TO NEW TECH COLD WAR

MAY 21, 2019

Photos: AFP

When US President Donald Trump signed a sweeping executive order to designate Huawei as a national security threat to America, he deepened the increasingly bitter trade conflict with China that threatens to irreversibly transform the two countries into mortal enemies. This single stroke of Trump's pen may have been one of the most consequential executive orders of his presidency and could have untold repercussions for America and the world for years to come.

Unlike previous moves against China, such as the arrest of Huawei executive Meng Wanzhou and the ZTE Saga, this latest attempt to choke Huawei, which is a national icon in China, will be perceived by the Chinese as an all-out war against them and crush any remaining illusions they may have about the possibility of an amicable resolution to the conflict. Trump's comment in an interview with Fox News that any deal with China cannot be 50/50 was another blunder. Trump and the American government are dangerously ignorant of China's culture.

The president's comment is bound to open fresh wounds and further provoke the Chinese. It is because the Chinese still retain vivid memories of the humiliating and unequal treaties imposed on them by Western powers in the 19th and 20th centuries. Trump's actions and remarks further reinforced the view among the Chinese that America is out to stop their rise. China wants to be treated as an equal by America, so any deal that disadvantages China will be a non-starter. A deal to end the trade war seems increasingly unlikely as the days pass.

And the fact that the president's policy received bipartisan support in Congress from Republicans and Democrats shows that anti-Chinese sentiment has spiralled out of control and translated into actual policy actions.

China has become the new bogeyman for the American political establishment to blame for all the problems facing the US.

However, for Sino-American ties to regrettably develop to this stage has been long in the pipeline, beginning with the entry of China into the World Trade Organization in 2001. The entry of hundreds of millions of Chinese workers has upended the world trading system and the American workforce is not prepared to deal with the challenges posed to them by the Chinese.

Many manufacturing jobs in the Rust Belt of America that provided livelihoods for many Americans for decades were lost as companies decided to outsource jobs to lower-cost countries like China and Mexico. And America under the wise leadership of president Bill Clinton had accumulated a huge budget surplus, which should have been put to good use through investments in infrastructure and education, which would have prepared America for the challenges of the 21st century. Instead, America became entangled in a mess in the Middle East after 9/11 under president George W Bush and squandered trillions of dollars.

China used this period to grow and develop its economy, which fuelled its rise.

While there are legitimate questions about some of the practices of the Chinese in terms of how they have conducted business, there is no doubt that the failure of American politicians to tackle structural reforms to revitalize their economy and prepare their people to face the challenges posed by the entry of China into the WTO in 2001 further exacerbated the consequences faced by low-wage American workers whose jobs have been outsourced overseas. America's political elites have failed to prepare their workforce to jump on the economic bandwagon propelled by the rise of China and India.

Let's be clear on this, even if the American government gets a trade deal with all the terms and conditions it wants, the challenges faced by America will not disappear and while highly educated Americans in places like Silicon Valley are well placed to take advantage of the rise, millions of Americans in Rust Belt states are poised to lose out and the haemorrhaging of jobs will continue despite a bid by Trump to stop it. The power of the presidency can only go to a certain extent against the power of economics.

Trump may think the Huawei ban will bring China to its knees and force it to beg for a deal, but he is wrong and we can expect Beijing to redouble its efforts to roll out a homegrown smartphone operating system alternative to Google Android. While China for years has had its own version of Twitter, Google and Facebook, there are still interlinks with American companies and as a result, China's progress translates into increased business for the Americans, too. Both sides win and there is an interdependent economic relationship. And businesses and people across the world benefit by using Chinese and American technologies together.

However, cutting out Huawei forces China to build from scratch a system that is totally independent of American technology. The Chinese and American economies will over time decouple from one another as the process of creating a digital iron curtain that separates the world into two distinct, mutually exclusive technological spheres gains momentum. Sooner or later, countries around the world may be forced to choose between the American Android system or a China alternative.

It is the beginning of a new cold war and the technological sphere is just one of the combat theaters.

China's government will pump in the funds needed to re-develop its industry and the Chinese may fail as they don't have the expertise of the Americans. But with time, the Chinese will be able to develop a comparable system to the one created by the Americans. And the US doesn't have the political will or ability to subsidize its own industry. Even if the US has the funds, it will be politically unpalatable due to the traditionally strong aversion of Americans toward government involvement with business sectors.

America may have the upper hand in technology, but Huawei is leading in the 5G race, so US supremacy may not continue forever. I will end by quoting Tim Culpan's Bloomberg article: "The winner won't be the side with the best fighters, but the one with the greater ability to endure the pain of prolonged losses."

AMERICA NEEDS TO RETHINK APPROACH TO IMMIGRATION

MAY 28, 2019

US President Donald Trump with Senator Tom Cotton. Photo: Zach Gibson/Pool via CNP

When US President Donald Trump spoke in the Rose Garden to outline his immigration policies to the American people, news broke that world-famous Chinese-American architect IM Pei had died. What a poignant situation it is for America, because the day Pei died, the country he chose to make his home introduced new proposals to tighten its immigration system.

America is known around the world as a beacon of hope, and millions of people aspire to get into the country to have a shot at the American dream. Immigrants like Ieoh Ming Pei emigrated to America with a dream and in the process, they enriched American culture and made America a stronger country. America should welcome more immigrants instead of closing its doors. While there are issues with illegal immigration, a specific solution is far more effective than a blanket solution that will shut the door to legal law-abiding immigrants.

Wars in the new era are fought in the economic sphere, so having talented citizens is what really determines the fate of countries. Many of America's greatest companies, such as Google, have been co-founded by immigrants and without these immigrants, America will be a weaker state.

However, in spite of all that has been said, and no matter how you feel about Trump, there can be little doubt that the president genuinely has good intentions. You may disagree with his policies but you can't deny that he genuinely feels he is doing what is best for America.

One factor contributing to America's dysfunctional political system is that politicians on both sides of the political aisle have failed to listen to each other. The rise of cable TV has given birth to 24/7 cable politics and it encourages both political parties to demonize the other. This is encouraged and enflamed by the media reporting on both sides of the political spectrum, be it Fox News or CNN.

As a result, American politics have become extremely toxic over time, and politicians who are willing to compromise are demonized and sidelined within the political system itself. The politics of consensus have gradually broken down at the very time that America needs its political system to work to enable the country to face up to the challenges of the 21st century.

The Republican, Democrat and independent politicians each have their own set of proposals on how to fix America's immigration system. There can be no question that many of them are patriotic Americans and they just want the best for their country. However, a lack of consensus prevents any enactment of meaningful immigration reforms.

And the delay in enacting reforms is costly for the US as its immigration system is severely overtaxed despite congressional approval to raise the cap on the number of immigration judges that can be appointed. The Justice Department has been unable to keep up with the hiring and there is an insufficient number of judges to process cases. This result is years of backlog in processing cases and migrants are released while waiting for a hearing. This is what the critics have called the catch-and-release policy, a policy that angers many Republicans, including President Trump, as a minority of these migrants either fail to turn up for their hearing or commit crimes. A study conducted by the NGO Human Rights First found that 8% of asylum seekers failed to turn up for their court hearing. And the majority of the illegal immigrants in America are people who have legally entered the country and then decided to overstay.

A lasting solution is needed to solve this crisis and for a start, there is a need to have a common federal and state policy on dealing with illegal immigrants. It doesn't help to have Democrats declaring their cities to be sanctuaries for illegal aliens and refusing to work with the federal authorities. While it is not illegal to seek asylum in the US, the majority of the people who are in the US illegally enter via legal channels. The Democrats may have a lot to say about Trump's immigration policy, but if you take a closer look at their statements, they have never questioned Trumps call to have a strong border.

On the website Portside, the academic Mark Tseng-Putterman

said, "Democratic rhetoric of inclusion, integration, and opportunity has failed to fundamentally question the logic of Republican calls for a strong border and the nation's right to protect its sovereignty."

Democrats and Republicans need to reach a consensus to forge a common nationwide policy. American politicians need to stop demonizing one another and put the interests of the country first.

And when Democrats and Republicans demonize one another on the campaign trail, the situation at the border continues. Both sides need to work together to solve this crisis, which is hurting everyone. They rallied together to save the economy during the 2008 financial crash, and I hope politicians can muster the same courage to solve the immigration crisis.

Another part of the solution that is equally essential but lacking is addressing the root cause of the crisis. Many of the reforms implemented by the US government over the past several decades have addressed the symptoms of the crisis, such as when the Reagan administration granted illegal immigrants legal status in the 1980s. Hence there is a recurring crisis which will time and time again demand the attention of policymakers in Washington.

And the majority of migrants now come from the Central American countries known as the Northern Triangle – El Salvador, Guatemala and Honduras. Many of these migrants have escaped poverty and violence in their countries and the responsibility lies at the doorstep of the United States.

Decades of US intervention in Central America, such as backing military coups and economic intervention, have destabilized the region. The very sight of these asylum seekers arriving at the doorstep of the US to seek asylum is a stark reminder to America of its disastrous interventionist policies in Central America. It also doesn't help that Trump cut off economic aid to the Northern Triangle, which will only worsen the problem.

So America needs a two-pronged strategy. In addition to reforming its immigration system, it needs to change its foreign policy toward the region. What the Northern Triangle needs is stable governance and economic development and the flow of asylum seekers will continue until these two elements are in place.

Stable but not necessarily 100% pro-American governments in the Northern Triangle are in the best interest of America. America needs a fundamental review of how it exercises its power in the region.

TRUMP SHOULD EXTEND HAND OF FRIENDSHIP TO TEHRAN

MAY 30, 2019

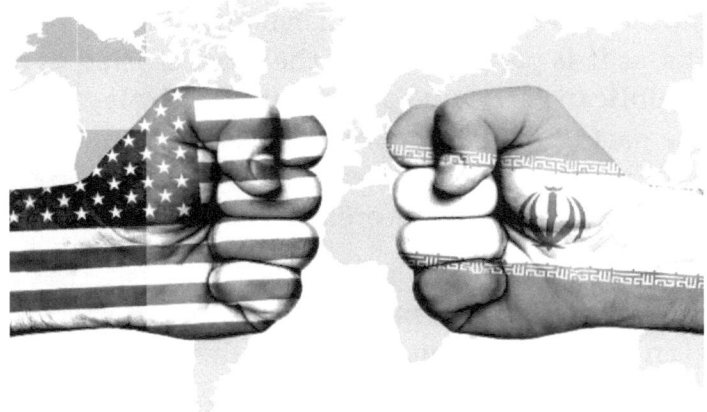

Image: iStock

I remember watching the Republican debate held in South Carolina in February 2016, when Trump was asked whether he thought former president George W Bush should have been impeached for his role in the Iraq war. Trump did not answer the question, but said, "The war in Iraq – we spent $2 trillion, thousands of lives, we don't even have it. Iran is taking over Iraq with the second-largest oil reserves in the world. So George Bush made a mistake. We can make mistakes, but that one was a beauty. We should not have gone into Iraq, we have destabilized the Middle East."

Trump absolutely nailed it when it comes to the Middle East. By removing Iraqi dictator Saddam Hussein from power, the US created a power vacuum in Iraq and destabilized the previously precariously power balance between the Sunni bloc led by Saudi Arabia and the Shia bloc led by Iran. The US spent trillions on the "war on terror" in the Middle East and incurred thousands of casualties, while infrastructure crumbled back home. Trump was right when he said there should not be any more nation-building abroad.

For Trump even to question the Bush family carried notable political risks, as it is perhaps one of the most storied dynasties in the US Republican Party. And questioning Bush's legacy cut to the core of the party's soul. The party prides itself on championing a strong military force and projecting US power overseas to protect and advance American interests.

However, in the end, many voters decided that they had had enough of the establishment, and Trump won the Republican nomination and subsequently the presidency. American voters are tired of foreign military interventions, and Trump's election was a clear reflection of that.

Since he became president, Trump has shown that he has no stomach for foreign military interventions and has tried to withdraw US forces from Syria and Afghanistan.

However, if he is not careful, he may find himself following in the footsteps of his predecessors and starting a war with Iran.

And in spite of the rising tensions resulting from such actions as the US withdrawal from the Iran nuclear deal, it is still possible for Trump to forge a different path and secure a legacy for himself. He himself is opposed to going to war in Iran, a position he re-affirmed during his remarks in his recent state visit to Japan.

Trump has repeatedly refused to be swayed by his advisers and instead acted on his instincts. This is admirable, but it can be a double-edged sword if not done correctly.

Unlike any other US presidents in modern memory, Trump can afford to change his policy positions without paying any polit-ical price. Many Americans voted for Trump because they wanted something different, and they do not expect things to stay the same. As well, Trump has a history of flip-flopping on his pos-itions, so there is a clear precedent.

Take North Korea as an example. Trump repeatedly clashed with its leader Kim Jong Un during the early days of his presidency. He even threatened to destroy North Korea in his first speech to the United Nations in September 2017. Kim fired back, even nick-naming Trump "Dotard."

But then something amazing happened. In a short span of a few months leading up to their historic meeting in Singapore in June 2018, the tone between Trump and Kim changed dramatically. And after the historic Singapore Summit, Trump praised Kim as very smart and very talented. The two men exchanged letters and even held a second summit in Hanoi in February of this year.

Even though the Hanoi summit failed, it is obvious that the im-pact of these two meetings has been very positive. It definitely lowered tensions in the Korean Peninsula and both sides have an interest in making diplomacy work and keep talking. One very good example of that is Trump contradicting his advisers on May 26 by playing down the impact of the North Korean missile tests conducted during his state visit to Japan.

Trump has upended decades of US policy on North Korea and set a new direction forward. With American voters wary of another military intervention, it will be very hard for future US presidents to overturn Trump policy on North Korea.

Now is the time for Trump to do the same thing with Iran. The US has vast cultural influence in Iran, but it has not been using it to its full advantage. Younger generations of Iranians are avid consumers of US movies and music. Despite bans by the Iranian government, Hollywood movies are easily accessible on the streets of Tehran for about a dollar apiece through digital pirating. A generation of young Iranians has grown up familiar with American culture.

And younger Iranians are more ideologically moderate and cosmopolitan than their parents' generation. They know what is going on outside Iran and they have been bravely fighting to bring their country in line with the modern era. Many young Iranians aspire to live in peace with the US, and Trump should know that the current Iranian regime doesn't represent those aspirations. Iranians below the age of 30 constitute the majority of the population and represent the future of the country.

Iran's current reformist president, Hassan Rouhani, who represents young Iranians, has been fighting a losing battle to maintain a moderate approach toward the outside world as the conservative forces led by Supreme Leader Ayatollah Ali Khamenei have gained ground since the election of Trump. By scrapping the approach of his predecessor Barack Obama, Trump has stymied the rise of reformist political factions within Iran who would have had a fighting chance of taking control of the country, heralding a new era.

Throughout history, some of the greatest turnarounds have come from within countries, not from outside. Attempts by reformist outsiders to intervene have often ended in failure. Take China, for example: its current reformist path is credited to its late leader Deng Xiaoping. US president Richard Nixon even made a trip to

China and laid the groundwork for the present Sino-US relationship.

The US should pay heed to its experiences in Vietnam, Afghanistan and Iraq. A confrontation with Iran would be no different.

Trump has made it very hard for any Iranian leader who wants to seek peace with the US. He wants to neutralize the threat of Iran, and this is not the way to go.

Trump should graciously extend a hand of friendship to Iran and resume the Obama-era approach toward the country. If Japan and the US, which were once the fiercest of enemies during World War II, can be the closest of allies now, the same scenario can be imagined for the US and Iran, which were once staunch allies before the 1979 Islamic Revolution.

President Nixon did a Nixonian approach with China, and it is high time for President Trump to do a Trumpian approach with Iran.

ASEAN SHOULD WEIGH IN ON TRADE DISPUTE

JUNE 4, 2019

Singaporean Prime Minister Lee Hsien Loong (center), Chinese Premier Li Keqiang (left) and Thai Prime Minister Prayut Chan-Ocha wait onstage for a group photo before the ASEAN-China summit on the sidelines of the 33rd Association of Southeast Asian Nations summit in Singapore on November 14, 2018. Photo: AFP / Lillian Suwanrumpha

ASEAN Summit 2019 is special because it will be held in June, much later than in previous years. Previous summits were normally held in April, but special accommodation was made for Thailand, this year's summit host, as it grappled with the formal coronation of King Vajiralongkorn and the formation of a newly elected government.

Perhaps everything happens for a reason, and this year's summit couldn't have been more perfectly timed. It will take place against the backdrop of an increasingly bitter trade war between the US and China. Trade talks have broken down between the two big powers and they have slapped additional tariffs on each other. China is looking into additional retaliatory actions such as the creation of unreliable foreign entities to retaliate against the US decision to ban Huawei from operating with American companies.

Hence this year the ASEAN Summit takes on a greater significance compared with previous years. It is an opportunity for ASEAN to demonstrate its relevance in this climate of mistrust between China and US that threatens the security of the world, including Southeast Asia.

It has been an open secret that ASEAN has been divided for years as the US and China tussle for influence in the bloc. And this division prevents ASEAN from coming together as one collective bloc in the face of important international developments, to its own detriment.

One notable event was the 2016 ruling by a tribunal in The Hague in favor of the Philippines in its case against China. However, in the ASEAN Statement of that year, any paragraphs that mentioned the case were removed, as ASEAN requires unanimous consent among its member states before a statement is released.

Cambodia and Laos, which are known to be close to China, firmly opposed any mention of the case in the statement.

This infuriated other countries such as Vietnam that have grave reservations over Chinese expansionism in the South China Sea. The development has laid the groundwork for a deep split within ASEAN that threatens to undermine the relevance and effectiveness of the bloc.

And now with rising tension between China and the US, it is time for ASEAN members to cast all divisions aside and unite as a bloc to present itself as a rational voice on this matter.

For this year's summit, ASEAN should release a joint statement calling on the US and China to resolve the dispute in a calm and peaceful manner.

As Singaporean Prime Minister Lee Hsien Loong has said, "When the lines start to get drawn, everybody asks, are you my friend or not my friend? And that makes it difficult."

This dispute has real-life implications for ASEAN as all of its members want to be friends with the US and China. And the conflict is bound to make the current arrangement increasingly unsustainable.

As the US has led an international effort to curb Huawei, countries including Japan and Australia have signed up to American initiative. But Malaysian Prime Minister Mahathir Mohamad has rejected attempts to exclude Huawei, saying his country will use the Chinese firm's technology as it deems fit. This is very important, because Malaysia has rejected the US attempt to drag it into America's efforts against China. It is very important for ASEAN to reject such attempts and avoid unwittingly contributing to the worsening of the conflict.

If ASEAN doesn't come together as one bloc and pull its weight on the US-China trade dispute, this worst-case scenario has every chance of being realized.

In the coming days, China and the US are bound to try to influence individual member states of ASEAN to come to their side. The member states should reject such manipulation and stand firmly as one bloc to oppose the march toward a new Iron Curtain.

ASEAN worked its magic in the aftermath of the Vietnamese invasion of Cambodia to prevent its legitimization. It is time for

ASEAN to work that magic again.

IN MALAYSIA, IT'S THE SAME OLD SEX STORY

JUNE 18, 2019

Anwar Ibrahim (center) meets supporters after submitting his documents at the nomination center for the by-election in Port Dickson, Malaysia, on September 29, 2018. Photo: Andalou Agency via AFP/Adli Ghazali

When news broke that Malaysian Economic Affairs Minister Azmin Ali had been accused of having a sexual relationship with a man, which is illegal in Malaysia, seasoned observers of the country's political scene were not surprised.

After all, we had been here before, Malaysian prime-minister-in-waiting Anwar Ibrahim was accused of sodomy after falling out with Mahathir Mohamad in 1998. He was subsequently convicted and jailed. Anwar has consistently claimed innocence and maintained the charges were designed to end his political career.

And this latest accusation against Anwar Ali is a sign of a well-concocted political conspiracy against him. And those who are familiar with developments in the People's Justice Party (PJP), which both Anwar and Azmin emerged from, should not be surprised by the saga.

But who is out to get Azmin? What is the purpose of doing all this?

Well, this saga has long been in the pipeline and is the consequence of the boiling over of months of tensions between the Azmin and Anwar camps. I dare say that it was the decision by Prime Minister Mahathir to appoint Latheefa Koya as chief of the Malaysian Anti-Corruption Commission (MACC) that led Azmin's detractors to make their move.

It is an open secret that the relationship between Azmin and Anwar went south a long time ago and they have made no effort to conceal it.

For example, back in March when Anwar's daughter Nurul called Mahathir a dictator and slammed his government for its slow delivery on campaign promises, Anwar rushed to play down his daughter's words and said his whole family still supported the prime minister.

However, instead of helping party president Anwar to douse the fire, Economic Minister Azmin, who also happens to be the deputy president of the PJP, decided to inflame the situation further by tweeting, "This country needs doers who are prepared to tough it out all the way, not cry-babies. Whatever it takes, we must make it work. If you can't take the heat, get out of the kitchen."

This tweet is widely seen as a swipe against Nurul Anwar and is a clear sign that the two men are at odds with each other.

Azmin is mistrusted by many allies of Anwar, who resented his close ties with Mahathir. When Anwar was still in the United Malays National Organization (UMNO) and held the position of deputy prime minister, Azmin, Anwar's principal private secretary, was known to be close to Mahathir. This fact was further confirmed by Azmin himself.

In a September 2018 speech to party members, Azmin revealed that his relationship with Mahathir went back a long way and he even called Mahathir "Uncle" in private. He revealed that Mahathir even attended his wedding and introduced him to Anwar.

Hence when Azmin decided to side with Mahathir and attacked Nurul Anwar, many pro-Anwar supporters viewed the incident as a further confirmation of Azmin's disloyalty to Anwar.

There are clear signs of lingering mistrust between the Mahathir and Anwar camps, and Mahathir's decision to appoint Azmin to the position of economic affairs minister after winning the 2018 Malaysian general election caught many in the Anwar camp wrong-footed. Azmin has proved himself to be a capable leader since he assumed the cabinet position and is seen by many as a potential future prime minister.

Many supporters of Anwar have suspected that Mahathir is out to derail Anwar's rise to the premiership despite the former's repeated assurances that he will honor his campaign promise to hand over power to him in 2020.

Another big factor in why they viewed Azmin as a threat to Anwar is the former's experience and age. Azmin is 16 years younger than Anwar and accumulated vital governing experience as chief minister of Selangor, Malaysia's richest state, from 2014 to 2018) and in his current position as economic affairs minister. Azmin would have been a good choice to succeed Mahathir as prime minister to lead the new Malaysia into the future.

Anwar, on the other hand, is already 71 years old and his last job with the government was in 1998 as deputy prime minister. His impending ascension to the premiership is bound to raise awkward questions regarding his ability to lead Malaysia into the next chapter.

Hence when Prime Minister Mahathir appointed staunch Anwar critic Latheefa Koya as the MACC chief commissioner, it was seen by many in the Anwar camp as a move by Mahathir to check Anwar. Many Anwar supporters also fear that Azmin will be elevated to higher positions should Mahathir decided to reshuffle his cabinet. Hence the divide in the PJP is deep-rooted and doesn't bode well for the future of the ruling coalition as the PJP is the biggest party in the Pakatan Harapan coalition.

And quite interestingly, Muhammad Haziq Abdul Aziz, the man who has accused Azmin Ali, is the senior private aide to Deputy Primary Industries and Commodities Minister Shamsul Iskandar. Shamsul is a firm ally of Anwar and he rallied behind him after Azmin questioned his decision to make several party leadership appointments in the aftermath of the party's 2018 internal election. Aziz also interned with the office of then minister Datuk Seri Nancy Shukri prior to Barisan Nasional's defeat in the 2018 general election.

And after the saga broke, allies of Anwar urged Azmin to go on leave pending the completion of the investigation and called on Mahathir to set a clear timetable to hand over power. Once you link all these points together, it is hard not to deduce that there is probably a conspiracy between the Anwar faction and the opposition to bring about the downfall of Azmin. However, Anwar has denied that his camp was behind the video.

Aziz even dared Latheefa to investigate him and Azmin, prompting Latheefa to announce that she will not be the one leading the investigation. Aziz knows that Latheefa and Azmin are firm political allies and he knows that having Latheefa leading the investigation would invite accusations of bias and political interference that would further smear Azmin's political reputation.

Anwar himself has stood by Azmin and rejected the accusations as gutter politics. However, seasoned observers will note that his support for Azmin is not 100% unconditional as he said, "We also fully support investigations by the police and the Malaysian Anti-Corruption Commission (MACC) in this case and hope that the processes can be carried out fairly and carefully,"

And having been investigated and charged with sodomy before, Anwar himself will know that drawing the MACC and police into it will lead Azmin to be implicated in a lengthy legal investigation even if it proves Azmin is innocent. Ironically, this clears the pathway for Anwar to take over the top job in 2020 with no credible opponent.

Hence this entire Azmin saga is the ugly manifestation of a bitter internal power struggle between the Anwar and Azmin factions in the PJP as the 2020 deadline for Mahathir to hand over power to Anwar nears. And this saga carries grave implications for the stability of the Pakatan Harapan government.

This doesn't bode well for Pakatan Harapan or Malaysia, as the PJP may splinter and this saga may be the beginning of the end of the Pakatan Harapan government.

US HAS NO MORAL RIGHT TO COMMENT ON EXTRADITION

JUNE 25, 2019

Protest organizers said almost two million people took part in a mammoth June 16 protest march against a proposed bill allowing for extradition to mainland China; city officials put the figure at around 300,000. Photo: Nile Bowie

Thanks to the street power of the people of Hong Kong, the government was backed into a corner and forced to suspend indefinitely a planned bill that would have authorized extradition to mainland China.

Hong Kong Chief Executive Carrie Lam apologized to Hongkongers with "utmost sincerity and humility" over the controversy caused by the extradition bill. Although she has refused to withdraw the bill outright, the very fact that it has been suspended is a huge victory for the demonstrators.

After all, the main motivation of the demonstrators to take to the streets in the first place was to pressure the Hong Kong government to make a U-turn on its intention to create a legal avenue for the extradition of criminal suspects to the mainland. Many critics of the bill have raised valid concerns, and they have made their opinions heard in the Hong Kong way.

However, it is worrying that throughout this saga, the bill's opponents seem to have thrown their principles out the window and blindly solicited support from outside powers such as the United States.

An example is Martin Lee, founder of Hong Kong's opposition Democratic Party, who met with US Secretary of State Mike Pompeo on May 16. Pompeo subsequently released a statement to express US concerns over the bill.

While I understand many have traditionally held the United States in high regard for its democratic norms and traditions, I hope Hong Kong political activists will realize that the US is no saint either and definitely not a credible friend of their cause. The US has no moral ground from which to comment on the extradition bill, and its actions throughout the saga reek of hypocrisy.

The actions of the United States in the past few years have proved that its rhetoric on upholding human rights, protecting the right to political dissent and respecting the will of the people has been nothing but words.

While the United States loves to put on its self-righteous hat and lecture others on how to manage and run their internal affairs, the US government has failed to listen to its own people and examine itself.

In the past few years, Americans of all walks of life have co-founded organizations like Black Lives Matter to protest police brutality that disproportionately impacts the African-American community. Politicians in the US, especially at the state level, pass gerrymandering laws to ensure their representatives continue to win elections for years to come.

Federal lawmakers in both main parties have failed to work together and are engrossed in political infighting that has incurred great costs for the average American. The lawmaking process has, in essence, ground to a halt in Washington, and many Americans don't trust their elected representatives to act in their best interests. This is backed up by a finding from Pew Research Center: "Only 17% of Americans today say they can trust the government in Washington to do what is right "just about always" (3%) or "most of the time" (14%)."

The US has many problems of its own and its political leadership has failed its own citizens.

If the memory of the Hong Kong activists still serves them well, they should remember the 2013 Edward Snowden incident that thrust Hong Kong into the global spotlight.

Snowden, a former US government contractor, fled to Hong Kong after leaking thousands of top-secret files that exposed a secret US government mass surveillance program targeting its own citizens and allies.

One of the damning revelations that the world came to know about was the existence of a secret court order that allowed the National Security Agency (NSA) to collect telephone records of all the customers of all US phone companies. The US government indiscriminately collects communication records of millions of its citizens regardless of whether they are suspected of any wrongdoing.

The US government was forced to make major reforms to assuage the massive outpouring of domestic and international outrage in the aftermath of the revelations.

Snowden did the world and the American people a big favor, and yet he is pursued by the US government for breaking national-security laws. The US exercised its right to request that Hong Kong hand Snowden over under the US-Hong Kong Extradition Treaty signed in 1997. Hong Kong refused, and he subsequently left the city and was granted political asylum by Russia. The US was displeased and told China it had undermined their bilateral relationship.

China did not hand over Snowden and thereby saved him from likely US imprisonment. Did the Hong Kong political activists give China due credit for this?

Opponents of the extradition bill claimed China would use the law to nail political dissidents. However, isn't the US guilty of the very same accusation? The US, which the Hong Kong pro-democrats have held in high regard, used the extradition treaty in their failed attempt to get Snowden.

And the recent arrest of Julian Assange, founder of WikiLeaks, is worth pondering for many.

Assange had taken refuge in the Ecuadoran Embassy in London since 2012 to avoid being extradited to the United States. WikiLeaks with the help of whistleblowers like Chelsea Manning published hundreds of thousands of top-secret US government files that showed US misdeeds like the alleged indiscriminate killing of civilians in Afghanistan and Iraq by US troops.

These revelations angered the US and it filed charges against Assange, which forced him to seek refuge in the embassy, where he stayed until his arrest by British police early this year when Ecuador revoked his refuge protection as it strove to reach a trade deal with the US.

Shortly after his arrest, the US sent an extradition request to the

UK, and his extradition hearing is set to begin in February 2020.

These two examples suffice to prove that the United States is guilty of prosecuting political dissidents that have hurt its interests. Aren't the Hong Kong activists aware of the implications of being associated with a foreign power that is guilty of all the accusations they have made against China?

What does this show? Wouldn't it damage their image and expose them as political opportunists who will align with anyone who aid their cause without any regard for their past?

Should they expose the dirt on the US in the future, can they be sure that Washington won't go after them?

I hope Hong Kong political activists will be more prudent in their future approaches, and that the US reflects on its own behavior before lecturing others on how to manage their affairs.

NOTES

1. https://www.asiatimes.com/2019/05/opinion/pakatan-harapan-must-not-rest-on-its-laurels/?_=7376742
2. https://www.asiatimes.com/2019/05/opinion/trump-china-and-the-art-of-no-deal/?_=7501393
3. https://www.asiatimes.com/2019/05/opinion/how-xi-and-abe-can-bridge-china-japan-divide/
4. https://www.asiatimes.com/2019/05/opinion/indonesia-must-address-creeping-islamization/?_=7585557
5. https://www.asiatimes.com/2019/05/opinion/washington-needs-a-nixon-moment-for-iran/?_=7121977
6. https://www.asiatimes.com/2019/06/opinion/asean-should-weigh-in-on-trade-dispute/?_=571742
7. https://www.asiatimes.com/2019/06/opinion/sex-allegation-threatens-to-destabilize-government/?_=1067824
8. https://www.asiatimes.com/2019/05/opinion/huawei-saga-is-prelude-to-new-tech-cold-war/
9. https://www.asiatimes.com/2019/05/opinion/america-needs-to-rethink-approach-to-immigration/